to

GW00602757

from

This edition copyright © 2003 Lion Publishing
Illustrations copyright © 2001 The Wright Sisters

Published by
Lion Publishing plc
Mayfield House, 256 Banbury Road,
Oxford OX2 7DH, England
www.lion-publishing.co.uk
ISBN 0 7459 4875 8

First edition 2001
1 3 5 7 9 10 8 6 4 2

Acknowledgments

Page 51: 1 Corinthians 13:5, 8; page 88: 1 John 4:18, taken from
the *Holy Bible, New International Version*, copyright © 1973, 1978, 1984
International Bible Society. Used by permission of Zondervan and Hodder
& Stoughton Limited. All rights reserved. The 'NIV' and 'New International
Version' trademarks are registered in the United States Patent and Trademark
Office by International Bible Society. Use of either trademark requires the
permission of International Bible Society. UK trademark number 1448790.

A catalogue record for this book is available
from the British Library

Typeset in Lemonade
Printed and bound in Singapore

Love is...
let me think!

Compiled by
Olivia Warburton

Illustrated by
The Wright Sisters

LION

If love is
the answer,
could you rephrase
the question?

Lily Tomlin

Most people
experience love
without noticing that
there is anything
remarkable about it.

Boris Pasternak

What is love?

Different people will give you different answers! In this book you'll find fun-sized definitions for love-spotters everywhere – what does love mean to you?

Puppy
love

I am not at all
the sort of person
you and I took me for.

Jane Carlyle

If I love you,
what does that matter
to you?

Johann Wolfgang von Goethe

There is no
safety net to protect
against attraction.

A.C. Swinburne

Come, woo me,
woo me; for now
I am in a holiday humour,
and like enough to consent.

William Shakespeare

It's very hard to
get your heart and
head together in life.
In my case, they're
not even friendly.

Woody Allen

Love can hope

where reason

would despair.

George, Lord Lyttleton

First
love

someone special

You!

Gavin Ewart

Love is a fan club
with only two fans.

Adrian Henri

We don't believe
in rheumatism and
love until after
the first attack.

Marie von Ebner-Eshcenbach

My heart has
made its mind up
And I'm afraid
it's you.

Wendy Cope

Love is

a great beautifier.

Louisa May Alcott

Unrequited love

lovesick

tears

look at me

I am two fools,

I know,

For loving,

and for saying so

In whining poetry.

John Donne

Love sought
is good, but
given unsought
is better.

William Shakespeare

Wooing, so tiring.

Nancy Mitford

There are very few of us
who have heart enough
to be really in love without
encouragement.

Jane Austen

There is nothing like desire
for preventing the things
one says from bearing any
resemblance to what one
has in one's mind.

Marcel Proust

Crazy
love

lots of fun

The human heart
likes a little disorder
in its geometry.

Louis de Bernières

If thou remember'st not
the slightest folly
That ever love did make
thee run into,
Thou hast not loved.

William Shakespeare

In dreams
and in love there are
no impossibilities.

Janos Arany

You call it madness,
but I call it love.

Don Byas

I'm sending you some kisses. I know you like them.

Anon

Romantic love

lovey-dovey

One is never too old
for romance.

Ingrid Bergman

Two souls with
but a single thought,
two hearts
that beat as one.

John Keats

Wherever you've got to
in the tunnel of love,
remember that some poet
has been there before you.

Daisy Goodwin

We all want to fall in love.
Why? Because that
experience makes us feel
completely alive.

Where every sense is
heightened, every emotion
is magnified, our everyday
reality is shattered and we
are flying into the heavens.

Anon

Cupboard
love

she
loves
me

he
loves
me

need you

If thou must love me,

let it be for nought

Except for love's sake only.

Elizabeth Barrett Browning

Give me a thousand kisses,
then a hundred,
then a thousand more.

Catullus

Constant togetherness
is fine – but only for
Siamese twins.

Victoria Billings

Every man I meet
wants to protect me.
I can't figure out
from what.

Mae West

Women were brought up to believe that men were the answer. They weren't. They weren't even one of the questions.

Julian Barnes

Self

love

big
hug

best
ever

one in a million

He that falls in love
with himself will have
no rivals.

Benjamin Franklin

Love is not self-seeking.

Love never fails.

The Bible

We had a lot in common.

I loved him and he loved him.

Shelley Winters

Love is mutually feeding
each other, not one living
on another like a ghoul.

Bessie Head

No woman has ever
shot her husband while
he was doing the dishes.

George Coote

Demanding love

be perfect

We do not judge
the people we love.

Jean-Paul Sartre

The difference between
friendship and love is
how much you can hurt
each other.

Ashleigh Brilliant

All love that has not
friendship for its base,
Is like a mansion
built upon the sand.

Ella Wheeler Wilcox

Relationships are like
sand held in your hand.
Held loosely, with an
open hand, the sand
remains where it is.
The minute you close your
hand and squeeze tightly

to hold on, the sand
trickles through your
fingers.

Kaleel Jamison

Tug of
love

to the bitter end

Love is a kind
of warfare.

Ovid

Love is
the bright foreigner,
the foreign self.

Ralph Waldo Emerson

The more I love,

the more I quarrel.

Marguerite d'Angoulème

A difference
of taste in jokes
is a great strain
on the affections.

George Eliot

I want to feel love
without making myself
vulnerable. I also want
to fly and not have to
leave the ground.

K. Bradford Brown

True
love

the one and only

True love is like
a pair of socks.
You gotta have two
and they gotta match.

Anon

If only one could tell
true love from false love
as one can tell mushrooms
from toadstools.

Katherine Mansfield

Truly loving another
means letting go
of all expectations.
It means full acceptance.

Karen Casey

No one is ever
betrayed by true love.

Jaufré Rudel

True love doesn't have
a happy ending. True love
doesn't have an ending.

Anon

Committed love

for ever and ever

Will you still love me
when I'm sixty-four?

Paul McCartney

Love is not love
that alters when it
alteration finds.

William Shakespeare

I know a lot of people didn't expect our marriage to last – but we've just celebrated our two months' anniversary.

Britt Ekland

Immature love says:
'I love you because
I need you.'
Mature love says:
'I need you because
I love you.'

Erich Fromm

Love takes time.
It needs a history
of giving and receiving,
laughing and crying.

Barb Upham

Unconditional love

be you

Love is unconditional.
Relationships are not.

Grant Gudmundson

Love is wanting to do
what you don't want to do
because you want to.

Mike Yaconelli

'I will love you for ever,'
swears the poet. I find this
easy to swear too. 'I will
love you at 4.15 p.m. next
Tuesday': is that still as easy?

W.H. Auden

Love rejects the
question, 'What am I
getting out of this?'

John Powell

Real love is a pilgrimage.
It happens when there is
no strategy, but it is very
rare because most people
are strategists.

Anita Brookner

Divine
love

God smiles

Love simply IS.

Jill Harrison

To love another person is to see the face of God.

Herbert Kretzmer

Love is the power
that heals the soul
and mends hearts.

Jill Harrison

There is no fear
in love. Perfect love
drives out fear.

The Bible

Do you want me to tell you something really subversive? Love **is** everything it's cracked up to be. That's why people are so cynical about it. It really **is** worth fighting for.

Erica Jong

To love is to risk rejection.

To live is to risk dying.

To hope is to risk despair.

To try is to risk failure.

But risks must be taken.

Because one of the
greatest dangers
in life is to risk nothing.
Only those who risk all
that they cannot keep
to gain what they can
never lose are truly free.

Simon Reynolds

To love is

to receive a glimpse

of heaven.

Karen Sunde